Be My Friend...

You know too much!

Compiled by Evelyn Beilenson
Introduction by Barbara Paulding
Illustrated by Robin Pickens

PETER PAUPER PRESS, INC.
White Plains, New York

Illustrations copyright ©2009 Robin Pickens
for Robin Pickens Designs, Inc.

Designed by Heather Zschock

Copyright © 2009
Peter Pauper Press, Inc.
202 Mamaroneck Avenue
White Plains, NY 10601
All rights reserved
ISBN 978-1-59359-835-8
Printed in China
7 6 5 4

Visit us at www.peterpauper.com

You'll Always Be My Friend...
You know too much!

Introduction

If life's path was not illuminated by the flares of friendship, it would be a long and winding road. But as it is, true friendship brings a light step to the journey. It's about showing up, knowing what's important, and sharing triumphs and challenges—sometimes

without words. In this whole wide world, we're as frank and feisty as only real friends can be—and that has made all the difference.

A true friend is someone who thinks that you are a good egg even though he knows that you are slightly cracked.

BERNARD MELTZER

One loyal friend is worth ten thousand relatives.

Euripides

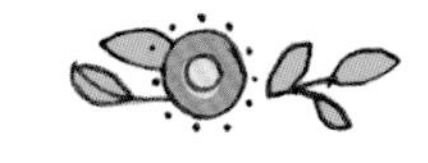

A faithful friend is
a strong defense:
and he that hath
found such an
one hath found
a treasure.

Ecclesiasticus 6:14

A true friend is
someone who
thinks that you are
a good egg even
though he knows
that you are
slightly cracked.

Bernard Meltzer

A friend is one before whom I may think aloud.

Ralph Waldo Emerson

True friendship
is like sound
health, the value
of it is seldom
known until
it be lost.

Charles Caleb Colton

I've always said
that in politics,
your enemies
can't hurt you,
but your friends
will kill you.

Ann Richards

One good reason
to only maintain a
small circle of friends
is that three out of
four murders are
committed by people
who know the victim.

George Carlin

What is a friend?
A single soul in two bodies.

Aristotle

It is the
friends you
can call up at
4 A.M. that
matter.

Marlene Dietrich

A friend is a gift you give yourself.

Baltasar Gracián

For You

If you want to win friends, make it a point to remember them. If you remember my name, you pay me a subtle compliment; you indicate that I have made an impression on you. Remember my name and you add to my feeling of importance.

Dale Carnegie

Never refuse
any advance of
friendship, for if
nine out of ten
bring you nothing,
one alone may
repay you.

Madame de Tencin

You can't
shake hands
with a
clenched fist.
Indira Gandhi

Wherever you are,
it is your own
friends who make
your world.

William James

Let us be grateful
to people who
make us happy;
they are the
charming gardeners
who make our
souls blossom.

Marcel Proust

This is
my beloved
and this
is my
friend.

Song of Solomon

Piglet sidled up
to Pooh from behind.
"Pooh!" he whispered.
"Yes, Piglet?"
"Nothing," said Piglet,
taking Pooh's paw.
"I just wanted to
be sure of you."

A.A. Milne

Love is the
only force capable
of transforming
an enemy
into friend.

Martin Luther King, Jr.

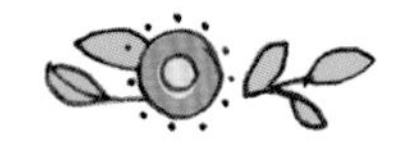

In everyone's life,
at some time, our inner
fire goes out. It is then
burst into flame by an
encounter with another
human being. We should
all be thankful for those
people who rekindle
the inner spirit.

Albert Schweitzer

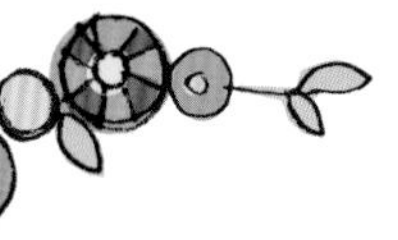

The essence of
true friendship
is to make
allowances for
another's little
lapses.

David Storey

It seems to me
that trying to live
without friends is like
milking a bear to
get cream for your
morning coffee. It is a
whole lot of trouble, and
then not worth much
after you get it.

Zora Neale Hurston

Friendship
is a
sheltering
tree.

Samuel Taylor Coleridge

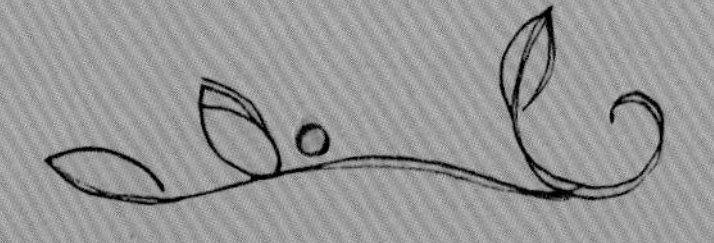

The best
mirror is an
old friend.
George Herbert

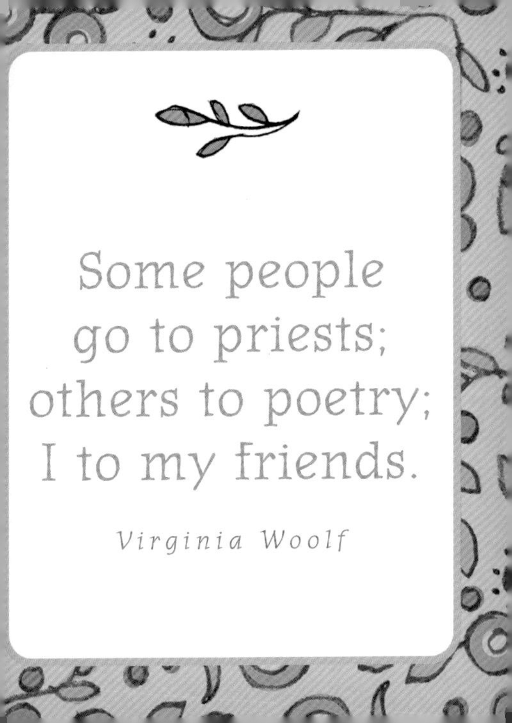
Some people
go to priests;
others to poetry;
I to my friends.
Virginia Woolf

I keep my friends
as misers do their
treasure, because,
of all things granted
us by wisdom,
none is greater
or better than
friendship.

Pietro Aretino

Treat your friends as you do your pictures, and place them in their best light.

Jennie Jerome Churchill

Friendship marks
a life even more deeply
than love. Love risks
degenerating into
obsession; friendship
is never anything
but sharing.

Elie Wiesel

Make new friends,
but keep the old;
Those are silver,
these are gold.

Joseph Parry

A brother may not be a friend, but a friend will always be a brother.

Benjamin Franklin

A friend is
one who believes
in you when you
have ceased to
believe in yourself.

Author unknown

Trouble shared is trouble halved.

Dorothy L. Sayers

A friend is one who knows us, but loves us anyway.

Father Jerome Cummings

Each friend
represents a world
in us, a world
possibly not born
until they arrive,
and it is only
by this meeting
that a new
world is born.

Anaïs Nin

A real friend
is one who
walks in when
the rest of the
world walks out.

Walter Winchell

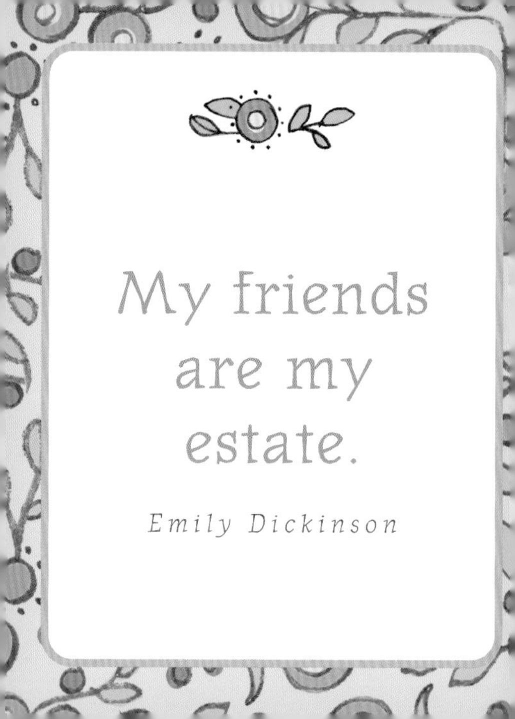
My friends
are my
estate.
Emily Dickinson

The road
to a friend's
house is
never long.

Danish Proverb

There is a magnet
in your heart that will
attract true friends.
That magnet is
unselfishness, thinking
of others first....
When you learn
to live for others,
they will live for you.

Paramahansa Yogananda

You can always
tell a real friend:
When you've made
a fool of yourself
he doesn't feel
you've done a
permanent job.

Laurence J. Peter

I've learned that
people will forget
what you said, people
will forget what you
did, but people will
never forget how you
made them feel.

Maya Angelou

A good friend is a connection to life—a tie to the past, a road to the future, the key to sanity in a totally insane world.

Lois Wyse

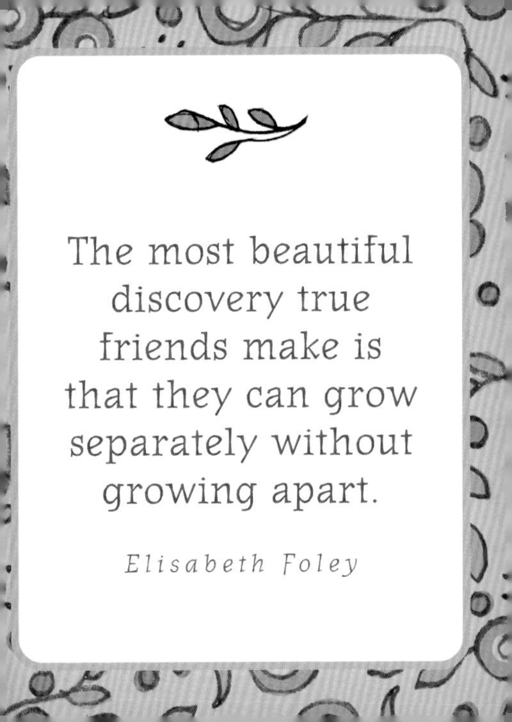
The most beautiful discovery true friends make is that they can grow separately without growing apart.
Elisabeth Foley

Good friends,
good books
and a sleepy
conscience:
this is the
ideal life.

Mark Twain

A true friend is one who overlooks your failures and tolerates your successes.

Doug Larson

A friend is
someone who
knows the song
in your heart,
and will sing it
back to you when
you forget
the words.

Author unknown

You meet people who
forget you. You forget
people you meet.
But sometimes you
meet those people
you can't forget.
Those are your friends.

Tennessee Williams

It is well, when judging a friend, to remember that he is judging you with the same godlike and superior impartiality.

Arnold Bennett

Remember, we all stumble, every one of us. That's why it's a comfort to go hand in hand.

Emily Kimbrough

The best way to
destroy an enemy
is to make him
a friend.

Abraham Lincoln

"Stay" is a
charming word
in a friend's
vocabulary.
Louisa May Alcott

Friends are like melons; shall I tell you why? To find one good you must one hundred try.

Claude Mermet

One who looks
for a friend
without faults
will have none.

Hasidic saying

Advice from
your friends is
like the weather;
some of it is good,
some of it is bad.

Author unknown

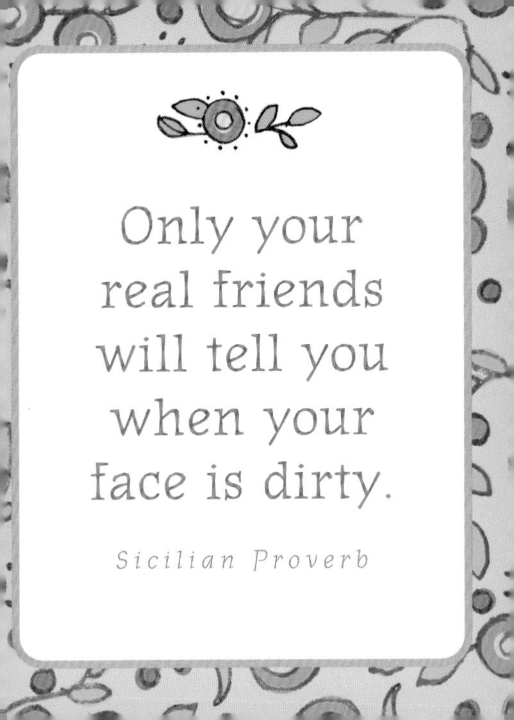
Only your
real friends
will tell you
when your
face is dirty.
Sicilian Proverb

Silences make the
real conversations
between friends. Not
the saying but the
never needing to say
is what counts.

Margaret Lee Runbeck

Laugh and the world laughs with you. Cry and you cry with your girlfriends.

Laurie Kuslansky

The friend who
holds your hand
and says the wrong
thing is made of
dearer stuff than
the one who
stays away.

Barbara Kingsolver

It takes a
long time to
grow an
old friend.

John Leonard

The greatest good you can do for another is not just to share your riches but to reveal to him his own.

Benjamin Disraeli

Love is blind,
but friendship
closes its eyes.

Proverb

A friend is someone
who sees through
you and still
enjoys the view.

Wilma Askinas

A hug is worth a thousand words.
A friend is worth more.

Author unknown

A true friend laughs
at your stories even
when they're not so
good, and sympathizes
with your troubles
even when they're
not so bad.

Irish Proverb

Friends are relatives you make for yourself.

Eustache Deschamps

A friend may well be reckoned the masterpiece of nature.

Ralph Waldo Emerson

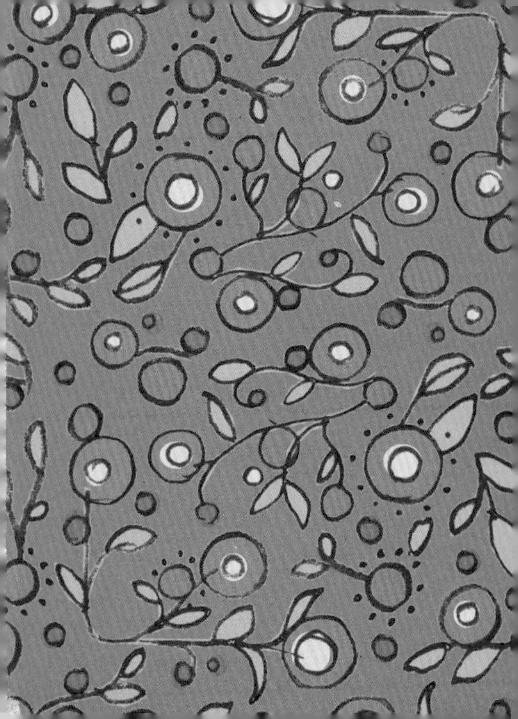

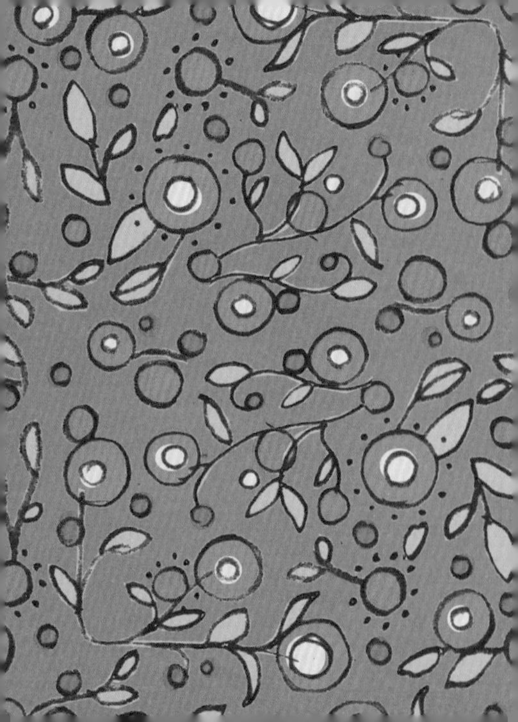